Bowls Cookbook for Beginners

365 Days of Easy and Delicious Recipes To Discover Healthy Combinations And Create Your Perfect Bowl With Nutritious Ingredients.

Berit Kranz

Table of contents

Chapter 5: Buddha Bowls

Chapter 6: Protein-Rich Bowls

Chapter 7: Vegan Bowls

Introduction

In the hectic pace of modern life, where time is of the essence, we frequently rely on quick and easy meals that do not necessarily meet our own health objectives. This is something that should not come as a surprise to anyone. Here are some things to consider: After a long and demanding day at work, you find that your stomach is rumbling by the time you get home. After spending a significant amount of time in the kitchen, the last thing you want to do is prepare a nutritious meal for your family. I am aware of the fact that there is contention, my friend. If I were to tell you that the answer is right in front of you, that there is a culinary trick that is just waiting to be discovered that has the potential to transform the way you cook and improve your health, what would you imagine? We hope that you have a wonderful time using the "Bowls Cookbook."

Bowls are the masters of ease of preparation, health, and flavor when it comes to the maze of flavors. If you lived in a world where cooking was not only a simple task but also a delightful culinary adventure, you would never have to worry about anything. As you delve deeper into the contents of this cookbook, you will come across the bowl-centric cooking approach, which has the potential to completely transform the way you think about food.

I would like to take you on a journey in which we acknowledge the challenges that we encounter on a daily basis, such as the tension that arises between our desire to have a lunch that satisfies our hunger and the constraints that we have on our time. I would like to take you on a journey in which we will acknowledge the difficulties that we encounter on a daily basis. The fact that you are experiencing this is not unique to you. Everyone has been there: staring into the void that is left by an empty refrigerator and wondering how possible it is to prepare a meal that is both delicious and nutritious without spending a significant amount of time in the kitchen. The Bowls Cookbook is here to assist you in your pursuit of a way of life that is both more convenient and more beneficial to your life and the lives of your family members. It makes sense of how you are feeling.

There are a multitude of benefits that come with cooking with bowls, and these benefits are significant and varied. It provides not only a means by which we can alleviate the stress that we all experience regarding time, but it also provides you with a blank canvas on which you can paint your culinary imagination. Imagine eating a dish that is a visual feast for the eyes and a sensory fiesta for your palate, bursting at the seams with brilliant colors, textures, and flavors. This is the kind of cuisine that you would want to eat. Bowls are not only pleasing to the eye, but they also provide a balanced and complete source of nourishment that is tailored to the needs of the body without compromising on flavor.

In the pages that follow, you will learn how to make bowls that are more than just a serving dish; rather, they are a celebration of a prosperous life. Whether you are a novice in the kitchen who is embarking on a culinary journey or an experienced cook who is looking to expand your repertoire, this book will serve as your guide. Recipes for a wide range of foods, including appetizers, main courses, and desserts, are included in this assortment. This section contains recipes that are experiences rather than just meals, where each mouthful takes you one step closer to becoming a more vibrant and healthy version of yourself.

With regard to the "Bowls Cookbook," what kinds of expectations does it have? You will learn how to quickly prepare meals that are both balanced and healthy, which is the first and most important thing you will learn. You should refrain from putting your health at risk in order to achieve greater convenience. Whether you're looking for hearty dinners or decadent breakfast bowls, this book has you covered. It guarantees that every meal you prepare is a step toward becoming a better and more vibrant version of yourself.

However, having a solid understanding of the recipes is only half the battle; the other half is having a deep understanding of the art and science of cooking, with a particular emphasis on bowls. Throughout the duration of this course, you will learn about the significance of providing your body with a healthy diet as well as the power that flavors have to balance our bodies. This is not just a cookbook; rather, it is a culinary guide that contains information that will enable you to make educated decisions about the foods that you put into your body based on what you put in your bowl.

It is likely that the question that is currently running through your head is, "Why should I trust the author of this cookbook to accompany me on this gourmet journey?" Your point of view is clear to me. The author is a seasoned food enthusiast who has not only mastered the technique of cooking with bowls but has also made it a way of life. Bowl cooking is a way of life. Although bowls are used for cooking, the author also uses them for eating. To create a collection of dishes that not only taste incredible but also improve your overall health, the author has spent years conducting research, making discoveries, and developing a profound understanding of the nutritional components that are present in human food. Because of this, the author was able to create this collection of works.

There is no use of specialized culinary terminology on these pages. Instead, you will find a companion who does not only share your goals regarding your physical well-being but also has the ability to relate to the challenges you face in the kitchen. It is not a distant expert who is providing guidance from a culinary ivory tower; rather, it is a friendly and approachable foodie who will say, "I've been there and can show you the way."

After you have finished reading "The Bowls Cookbook," you will find that you are nodding your head in agreement and telling yourself, "This is the book I actually ought to read." However, it is not simply a collection of recipes; rather, it is a guide to living a better and healthier life. Having this book in your possession will allow you to enter a world where every meal is a celebration of flavor and health. This book presents you with the opportunity to enter that world, regardless of whether you are a working professional, a parent who is juggling a multitude of responsibilities, or someone who simply wants to improve their cooking skills.

Prepare yourself for a gastronomic journey in which each dish will serve as a stroke of the brush for the artwork that will be your comfort meal, and the bowls will serve as a canvas for the artwork. It is more accurate to say that The Bowls Cookbook is a promise than a simple book. There is a guarantee that you can begin your journey toward meals that are both healthier and more delicious right here, right now. Let's dive in together and find out how cooking with a bowl as the focal point can completely transform the way you approach your favorite dishes.

Chapter 1: The Science Behind The Bowls Cookbook Diet

Unlocking nutritional balance: The cornerstone of cooking with bowls

When it comes to the numerous culinary options that are available, The Bowls Cookbook stands out as a beacon that is both flavorful and nutritious. This chapter delves into the scientific principles that underpin the Bowls Cookbook diet, as well as the concepts that make it a unique and practical approach to providing your body with fuel. The diet known as the Bowls Cookbook was developed by two medical professionals, David Katz, M.D. and F. Christopher Bland, M.D.

The strength of nutritional synergy: a balancing act

One of the most important aspects of cooking with bowls is mastering the art of balance, which refers to the intricate interaction of nutrients that goes beyond simple food consumption. In order to give the body the energy it needs, it is essential to focus on creating a nutrient symphony rather than simply adding items to the bowl.

Take into consideration a dish consisting of quinoa, which is a fantastic source of protein and contains all of the essential amino acids. You should incorporate a wide variety of colorful vegetables into the mixture; each of these vegetables will bring a different set of nutrients (minerals and vitamins) to the meal. The addition of a source of healthy fat, such as almonds or avocado, to this bowl results in a combination that not only satisfies your sense of taste but also provides you with a comprehensive range of nutrients.

The principle of nutritional synergy, which states that certain nutrients are more beneficial to health when taken together, is the scientific foundation upon which the balance that was mentioned earlier is based. To illustrate this point, one way to do so is to combine foods that are high in iron with foods that are high in vitamin C. There is evidence to suggest that this improves the body's ability to absorb iron. Due to the fact that vitamin C improves the body's capacity to absorb iron, you can be certain that your body is getting the maximum benefit from the nutrients that you consume. Every single ingredient that is included in the Bowls Cookbook was selected not only because of its own unique nutritional profile, but also because of how well it complements and enhances the nutritional content of the Bowls as a whole.

As a whole, flavors: the psychological mechanisms behind satisfying meals It is important to note that the research that underpins bowl-centric cuisine takes into account the psychology of eating in addition to nutrition. A meal should not merely be consumed as a means of warding off hunger; rather, it should be enjoyed as an experience that engages all five senses. The flavors that are included in the Bowls Cookbook are not haphazardly combined; rather, they are carefully arranged in such a way as to create a symphony of the senses that satisfies both the palate and the appetite. Think about the combination of the sourness of a citrus vinaigrette with the umami-rich flavors of vegetables that have been roasted. This is not merely a matter of taste; rather, it is an effort that has been made on purpose to stimulate your taste receptors and provide you with an experience that is satisfying. When flavors are combined in an inventive manner, the tongue's intricate dance of taste receptors is activated, and the result is that each mouthful becomes an enjoyable experience in and of itself. It is not as simple as a matter of personal preference.

The sensory experience is also enhanced by the presence of a variety of textures within a bowl, such as the crispiness of fresh vegetables, the smoothness of an avocado, and the chewiness of grains. The idea behind this is that eating a variety of foods that each have their own unique texture not only makes eating more enjoyable, but it also sends a message to the brain that you are consuming a meal that is substantial and satisfying. Intestinal health and the Bowls cookbook: helping to alleviate digestive discomfort

Maintaining excellent gut health is extremely important, and this is something that cannot be ignored when discussing healthier lifestyles. Instead of focusing solely on the foods that you consume, the Bowls

Cookbook diet takes into consideration how your body processes and utilizes the nutrients that it consumes. The method that is utilized in this context is the scientific method of selecting components that not only provide the necessary nutrients but also facilitate healthy digestion and absorption.

A significant number of bowl dishes place an emphasis on fiber because of its importance to the health of the intestines. The Bowls cookbook makes a conscious effort to incorporate all of these components, whether it be the soluble fiber that can be found in fruits and vegetables or the insoluble fiber that can be found in whole grains. Fiber serves as a prebiotic, which means that it strengthens the beneficial bacteria that are already present in the stomach. In addition to making meals heavier, which encourages fullness, fiber also serves as a prebiotic. In this context, the science that underpins this is fiber's capacity to do both.

Furthermore, fermented foods such as yoghurt or kimchi, which are frequently used in bowl recipes, contribute to the maintenance of a healthy microbiome in the gut system. The process of fermentation is a scientific method that simplifies the digestion of highly complex compounds by breaking them down into simpler forms. By doing so, the assimilation of nutrients is improved, and a harmonious environment in the intestinal tract is fostered.

Blood sugar harmony: a nuanced mixture of components

These individuals who are concerned about their blood sugar levels will find the Bowls Cookbook diet to be a friend and an ally. The science that underpins it encompasses the selection of components that have a low glycemic index, or those that raise blood sugar levels in a gradual and consistent manner. Whole grains, lean proteins, and an abundance of vegetables that are high in fiber are all things that are encouraged to be used in the Bowls Cookbook in order to assist in maintaining balanced blood sugar levels.

You might want to think about using quinoa as the base of a dish and then topping it with grilled chicken, beautiful greens, and cherry tomatoes. In addition to producing a surge of flavor, this combination also causes glucose to be released into the bloodstream after a gradual process. Both of these advantages are directly brought about by the combination. When it comes to bowl cuisine, the science that underpins the regulation of blood sugar is the deliberate selection of components that encourage a steady and balanced release of energy. The ups and downs that are brought on by careless eating patterns can be avoided by going about things in this manner.

The science of shells is always changing.

While we are coming to the end of our investigation into the scientific foundations of the Bowls Cookbook diet, it is essential to acknowledge that science is a dynamic and ever-expanding field of study. The term "bowl-centered cooking" refers to a cooking technique that exemplifies the delicate relationship that exists between the food that we consume and the way that our bodies function.

Each and every bowl that has been meticulously prepared tells a distinctly different story about the harmony of flavor, nutrition, digestion, and the regulation of blood sugar. Food science is a branch of science that embraces the concept that every component of a dish serves a purpose, and that purpose is to provide your body with nourishment that goes beyond simply satisfying your hunger.

It is important to keep in mind that using the Bowls Cookbook involves more than just cooking; it is similar to twirling with the laws of taste and nutrition. When you begin your journey through the world of cuisine with the Bowls Cookbook, it is essential that you are aware of this. Every bowl provides you with the opportunity to take pleasure in the harmony of flavors, the balance of nutrients, and the satisfaction of providing your body with nourishment that extends beyond the confines of the plate at the same time. You can take a step toward becoming a more vibrant and healthy version of yourself with each bite of food that you consume from The Bowls Cookbook. Here are some examples.

Chapter 2: What Is a Bowl?

In light of the fact that we are nearing the conclusion of our investigation into the scientific underpinnings of the Bowls Cookbook diet, it is essential to keep in mind that the scientific field is one that is dynamic and is always undergoing significant changes. An approach to cooking that is referred to as "bowl-centered cookery" draws attention to the intricate relationship that exists between the food that we consume and the way in which our bodies operate.

Each dish that has been expertly crafted tells a unique story about how the four aspects of flavor, nutrition, digestion, and blood sugar regulation are all in harmony with one another. The concept that each component of a meal serves a purpose, one that provides your body with profound nourishment rather than merely satiating your appetite, is one that is taken into consideration by this scientific discipline.

It is important to keep in mind that cooking with the Bowls Cookbook is not just about cooking; rather, it is like dancing with the rules of nutrition and taste. It is essential to have this information at your disposal when you start your journey into the world of cooking by using the Bowls Cookbook. Each bowl provides the satisfaction of providing your body with nourishment that extends beyond the confines of the plate, in addition to the harmony of flavors and the nutritional balance that it provides. It is possible that with each meal that you prepare from The Bowls Cookbook, you will make progress toward becoming a more vibrant and healthy version of yourself.

Where does the bowl lining come from?

Because of the bowl's resemblance to the round belly of the Buddha statue and the fact that its contents are supposed to have the effect of making people smile, the term "Buddha bowl" is said to have been given to the bowl. On the other hand, this is just one portion of the story. It is believed that the Buddha bowl originated in ryori, which is a culinary tradition that is associated with Zen Buddhism.

This one-of-a-kind practice that the monks engage in during mealtimes helps them develop an awareness of both the food and themselves. Every day, it is strictly forbidden for the monks to consume more food than they require for their bodies. In Buddhist monasteries and among Buddhists in general, this particular eating style is considered to be of great religious significance because it is considered to be a symbol of the transition from the role of student to the role of teacher.

On the other hand, the bowls initially gained popularity around the time that culinary bloggers realized they could use the diverse and colorful dishes as backdrops for their photographs. They have achieved worldwide renown as a consequence of this. Over the past few years, vegetarianism and bowls have practically become synonymous with one another's meaning.

Because they encourage eating a meal that is both healthy and well-balanced, the bowls gained immense popularity in a short amount of time. The eating pattern that is associated with this cooking trend has a significant impact on the structure of the body. People who have previously consumed unhealthy food will not only experience a significant change in their mentality, but they will also experience a reduction in their body weight. It is possible to actively support mental stability by increasing the proportion of high-quality foods in one's diet as well as the amount of nutrient-dense foods that individuals consume.

Those who take part in the rituals and practices that are associated with the act of eating stand to gain a great deal from the practices of mindfulness and meditation.

Buddha bowl kit

The Buddha dish does not contain any ingredients that come from animals. Because Buddhism is primarily a vegetarian religion, we no longer consider this to be a "typical" interpretation of ryuki, despite the fact that some contemporary versions include meat as a source of protein.

A Buddha bowl consists of the following components:

- 20 % carbohydrates

Rice, millet, sweet potatoes, quinoa, couscous, peas, potatoes, corn, amaranth, etc.

- 20 % proteins

Lentils, beans, chickpeas, edamame, tofu, quark, etc.

- 20 % vegetables

Zucchinis, broccoli, peppers, tomatoes, mushrooms, carrots, etc.

- 20 % salad

Swiss chard, spinach, savoy cabbage, lamb's lettuce, etc.

- 10 % fat

Avocado, nuts, chia seeds, olive oil, etc.

- 10 % Toppings

Foods such as sprouts, pumpkin seeds, sesame seeds, fruit, coconut flakes, feta cheese, and so on.

Due to the fact that these six components can be combined in a wide variety of different ways, you have the ability to experiment with an infinite number of different combinations. Whatever the case may be, the salad must serve as the foundation upon which the other components of the meal are built and seasoned according to personal preference. The practice of mindfulness and the nutritional content of the food are always the primary concerns of the food. The act of preparing food not only promotes enjoyment but also a more mindful approach to the act of eating.

Poke bowl kit

It is important to remember that fish is the primary ingredient in poke bowls. It is the most significant dietary source of protein and can also occasionally be used as fat. In little time at all, a basic Buddha bowl can be converted into a useful poke bowl.

The fish in the original poke bowls was consumed raw, much like in sushi or hoe deopbap, and the meal was only seasoned with a marinade. Ginger, lime, chile, and other herbs and spices are added to soy sauce, which serves as the marinade's primary ingredient.

Poke bowls, which were quite popular in Hawaii in the 1970s, are having a bit of a renaissance these days due to the popularity of the Buddha Bowl.

With the exception of the fact that the proteins and fat in the poke bowl can also be derived from seafood like salmon, herring, or prawns, the Buddha bowl and poke bowl have the same structure.

What makes the bowl so popular?

The growing popularity of bowl meals is not a coincidence. The cuisine is quite popular because it has many attractive ingredients. The food itself takes center stage first. a range of fresh foods that work well with different diets and lifestyles and are safe from a nutritional standpoint. To allow you to customize the bowls to your own eating preferences and habits, the structure is simply described in general terms.

You can make good use of leftovers from the prior day as well. This bowl has enough space for everything, whether you are serving cooked veggies or rice. In a comparatively short amount of time, the remaining bowl components can likewise be manufactured. As a result, a lot of caterers find it highly appealing to open shop there. Making bowls is simple and adds a whole new dimension to well-established kitchens by highlighting food that has only been lightly processed and returned to its natural state. Influencers may use this colorful, glowing bowl of various veggies as the perfect backdrop to showcase their brands without really being in the picture. Apart from the obvious visual attraction of healthy food, most people realize right away the plethora of other advantages that come with it.

A diet rich in a balanced combination of macro and micronutrients can uplift your spirits and excite your thoughts. A thoughtful and balanced diet can help to boost the immune system and prevent numerous diseases. Actively matching your diet to your body's requirements might help you focus better, feel less exhausted all the time, and even manage depressive episodes better.

The food within the bowl has been prepared with an emphasis on mindfulness. Here, there aren't many sauces or excessively prepared foods, so you can savor the food's flavor as you consume it. You should also be mindful of the food you consume. Even though it's a necessary aspect of every day, this has become nearly ordinary at this point. Bowl eating is frequently done in a contemplative manner, which aids in bringing attention back to the more important facets of everyday existence. It is possible to experience and assess previously completely automated processes afresh when they are consciously recognized. Stress hormones can now be processed more effectively thanks to the relatively recent realization that deceleration alters our perception of reality.

Bowl food is more than just a meal; it's a representation of a whole culture in which you can take part, fully or partially. Eating foods that are local to the culture allows you to learn about its elements, adapt them into your own lifestyle, and get the physical and mental benefits of a nutritious diet.

Chapter 3: Poke Bowls

1. Spicy salmon with spinach

Ingredients for 4 portions:

- Salt
- 400 g salmon fillet / peanut oil
- 200 g cooked rice / 100 g baby spinach
- 150 g cooked edamame
- Rice wine vinegar
- For the marinade:
- Black sesame seeds
- 50 ml soy sauce / 1 spring onion stalk
- 5 g rice wine vinegar / 2.5 g honey
- 5 g ginger / 5 ml sesame oil
- 5 g Sriracha
- For the mayonnaise:
- Dried chili flakes / 150 g light mayonnaise
- 2.5 g miso paste / 50 g sour cream

Preparation:

1. Wash the spinach, please. Make sure to grate the ginger.
2. Slice the spring onions lengthwise. Salmon should be cut into cubes. After combining all the marinade ingredients well, put the salmon in the refrigerator to marinate for 10 minutes.
3. In a bowl, combine all of the mayonnaise's ingredients. After adding the rice, give the container a little tap.

4. Drizzle it with a little marinade. Toss in the spinach along with a small amount of salt, rice vinegar, and peanut oil.
5. Arrange the salmon over the rice, along by the edamame and spinach. As a garnish, use mayonnaise and toasted sesame seeds.

2. Fruity and spicy tuna

Ingredients for 4 portions:

- Cress
- 400-450 g tuna / gari
- 1 avocado / olive oil
- 1 mango / 200 g quinoa
- For the marinade:
- Black sesame seeds
- 30 ml soy yogurt
- sweet soy sauce / 50 g shallots
- 5 ml sesame oil / 2.5 g garlic
- 2.5 g ginger
- For the yogurt:
- Salt
- 200 g Greek yogurt
- Juice and zest of ½ a lime
- 1-30 ml wasabi powder
- 1 garlic clove

Preparation:

1. Slice the avocado's flesh thinly after removing the stone.
2. Cut the mango into dice, pit it, and peel it.
3. Follow the directions on the package to prepare the quinoa. Grate the ginger. Peeling the garlic is necessary before grating it.
4. Slice the spring onions lengthwise. Trim and chop the shallots. To extract the juice, grate the lime zest.
5. Toss in the tuna and chop. After combining all the marinade ingredients well, place the tuna in the refrigerator to marinate for ten minutes.
6. Combine all of the yogurt's ingredients. Mix thoroughly after adding a small amount of salt and olive oil to the quinoa.
7. After putting the quinoa in a bowl, set it aside. Top with tuna,

avocado, and mango. The meal is garnished with yogurt, cress, sprouts, and other ingredients.

3. Fish salad with macadamia

Ingredients for 2 portions:

- Salt
- 300 g tuna / 5 ml honey
- 1 red onion / 15 g chili sauce
- 2 spring onions
- 15 ml sesame oil
- 15 g macadamia nuts
- 30 ml soy sauce
- 10 g sesame seeds

Preparation:

1. After cleaning, cut the tuna into cubes. Slice the onion into small strips after removing the skin. After washing, chop the spring onions into rings.
2. Chop the nuts and place them in a fat-free pan to be prepared.
3. After that, add and cook the sesame seeds. Take out both of them from the pan and leave them to cool.
4. Add a quarter of the chopped sesame seeds, onions, and almonds to the fish.
5. Then, using a whisk, thoroughly mix in the honey, oil, chili sauce, and soy sauce. After adding salt to taste, divide into individual bowls.
6. Lastly, add the remaining sesame seeds, almonds, and onions to the dish.

4. Salmon with avocado

Ingredients for 4 portions:
- Sesame seeds / 200 g cooked rice
- 60 g gari / 400 g salmon fillet
- 50 g dried seaweed / 2 avocados
- 100 g green onions
- For the marinade:
- 10 g lime juice / 30 ml soy sauce
- 5 ml sesame oil / 2.5 g ginger

Preparation:
7. Cut the avocado flesh into cubes after removing the stone. Slice the spring onions lengthwise. Finely grated the ginger. Salmon should be cut into cubes.
8. After combining all the marinade ingredients well, let the salmon sit in the marinade for 10 minutes at room temperature.
9. As directed on the package, prepare the seaweed by soaking it in water and letting it sit there. To serve, prepare the rice.
10. Arrange the seaweed, avocado, salmon, and gari on top.
11. Add the spring onions and a little of the marinade on top. Garnish with a handful of toasted sesame seeds and serve.

5. Tofu with rice and radishes

Ingredients for 4 portions:

- Daikon cress / 400-450 g natural tofu
- 6 radishes / 30 ml nori leaves
- 2 baby cucumbers / 200 g cooked rice
- For the dressing:
- 1 spring onion / 2 7.5 ml olive oil
- 30 ml wakame / 30 ml sesame oil
- 30 ml soy sauce / 30 ml yuzu juice
- 30 ml honey

Preparation:

1. Slice the nori sheets into strips. Cut the radishes and tiny cucumbers into thin slices. Make sure to grate the ginger.
2. Slice the spring onions lengthwise. Cube the tofu with a knife. After combining all the dressing ingredients well, set aside to marinate the tofu for 10 minutes before serving.
3. As soon as the rice is in the bowl, drizzle some of the dressing over it.
4. Arrange the cucumber, radish, and tofu in a pleasing manner over the rice. Garnish the meal with daikon cress and nori leaves.

6. Tuna with red cabbage

Ingredients for 4 portions:
- 6 radishes / 200 g cooked rice
- 2 cucumbers / 400 g tuna fillet
- Black sesame seeds / 50 g dried seaweed
- 1 avocado
- For the marinade:
- 10 ml lime juice / 30 ml soy sauce
- 5 ml sesame oil / 2.5 g ginger
- For the red cabbage:
- 15 g sugar / ½ head of red cabbage
- 15 g salt

Preparation:
1. Tuna should be cut into cubes and refrigerated. Cut the avocado flesh into wedges after removing the stone.
2. Slice the cucumber into tiny pieces. After washing, cut radishes into slices. Grate the ginger.
3. After all of the marinade ingredients have been well combined, put the tuna in the refrigerator for ten minutes.
4. Red cabbage should have its stalk removed and then chopped into small pieces. Next, add salt and sugar for seasoning.
5. In a bowl, combine all ingredients and let infuse for twenty minutes. After preparing the seaweed according to the directions on the package, let it expand.
6. Place the red cabbage, avocado, seaweed, tuna, and radishes on top of the rice in a bowl.
7. Drizzle it with a little marinade. Before serving, sprinkle the roasted sesame seeds over the meal.

7. Prawns with mango and lettuce

Ingredients for 2 portions:

- Coriander / 240 ml rice vinegar
- Sesame
- Pickled ginger
- 60 g sesame paste
- 4 limes / ½ avocado
- 5 g sugar
- 60 g wakame seaweed salad
- 5 g sugar / 1 mango
- 300 g peeled prawns
- 2 spring onions

Preparation:

1. Tear the lettuce into bite-sized pieces after giving it a good wash. Grate the lime zest in order to release the juice.
2. Bring the soy sauce's contents—rice vinegar, lime zest, lime juice, sugar, and sesame paste—to a boil.
3. Stir and let the mixture thicken for a further five minutes. Place the sauce in the refrigerator to cool it down. Peel and chop the mango into small pieces as you wait.
4. Slice the spring onions lengthwise. After removing the avocado's stone, chop the flesh into cubes. The pan's oil is heated. Deep-fry the prawns for a minute on each side in the heated oil.
5. When the sauce is ready, add the prawns. Spread out the salad after placing it in a bowl. Place the wakame seaweed salad, avocado, mango, and prawns on top.
6. Distribute the marinade evenly over the dish. Add some spring onions, sesame seeds, coriander, and pickled ginger before serving.

8. Tuna with carrots and avocado

Ingredients for 4 portions:

- Sesame seeds / 300 g brown rice

- 1 bunch coriander / 600 g raw tuna
- 2 avocado / 15 g soy sauce
- 3 carrots / 10 g sesame oil
- 2 spring onions
- 15 g rice wine vinegar
- 2 garlic cloves
- 1 ginger (1 cm)

Preparation:

1. Chop and peel the ginger and garlic. Slice the spring onions into rings. Toss in the tuna and chop.
2. Combine the vinegar, sesame oil, ginger, garlic, soy sauce, and spring onions to make a marinade.
3. While the tuna marinates in the sauce, place it in the refrigerator for at least one hour. Follow the directions on the package to prepare the rice.
4. After pealing, grate the carrots. For the preparation, chop the coriander. After removing the stone, chop the avocado's flesh.
5. Distribute the rice among four plates. Place the avocado, tuna, and carrots on top. As a garnish, mix in some toasted sesame seeds and fresh coriander.

9. Salmon cream with cucumber

Ingredients for 4 portions:

For the sauce:

- 1.5 g pepper / 80 g mayonnaise
- 2.5 g salt / 2.5 g mirin
- 1.5 g sugar / 15 g Siracha
- Oy sauce / 1 ginger (1 cm)
- For the poke:
- 300 g brown rice / 500 g salmon fillet
- 3 spring onions
- For the cucumber:
- 2.5 g chili flakes / 2 mini cucumbers
- 5 g salt / 120 ml rice vinegar
- 80 ml honey / 120 ml water

Preparation:

1. As directed on the package, prepare the rice according to the directions. After combining all the sauce components, let aside to cool.
2. There should be a separate set of rings on the white and green portions of the spring onions.
3. Dice the salmon into small pieces and combine it with the sauce and the white sections of the spring onions in a bowl. Bring the water, vinegar, salt, chili flakes, and honey to a boil in a small pan.
4. As soon as you're ready, slice the cucumber and put it to the saucepan. When the temperature is comfortable, about ten minutes later, take the cucumbers out of the stock.
5. For each person, put the rice in a different container. Place the cucumber and salmon in layers on top. Lastly, spoon the leftover sauce over everything and scatter the last of the spring onions over top.

10. Hot watermelon with nuts

Ingredients for 4 portions:
- Sprouts
- 1 watermelon without seeds / 1 bunch of coriander
- 1 spring onion / 1 avocado
- 2-3 cucumbers / 1 jalapeño
- 100 g macadamia nuts

For the dressing:
- 2.5 g sesame oil
- 15 g honey
- 10 g rice wine vinegar
- 10 g lime juice

Preparation:
1. Slice the spring onions into rings. Dice the little cucumbers into small pieces.
2. Cut the macadamia nuts into pieces. Dice the jalapeños into tiny pieces. After removing the stone, chop the avocado's flesh. Peel and grate the garlic to prepare it. Peel and cut the watermelon into pieces.
3. First, combine all the ingredients for the dressing and let it marinade the melon. Put in the refrigerator for a little.
4. In a bowl, combine the remaining ingredients. Pour the leftover marinade over the melon that has been marinated.
5. Before serving, garnish the dish with the coriander and sprouts.

11. Vegan fruit poke bowl

Ingredients for 3 people:

For the tofu:

- 1 lime / 400 g firm tofu
- 1.5 g chili garlic sauce
- 60 ml sesame oil / 5 ml sesame seeds
- 60 ml soy sauce / 1 ginger (1 cm)
- 30 ml pineapple juice / 15 g rice vinegar
- For the poke:
- Chives
- 200 g pineapple / 1 chili
- 1 avocado / 70 g quinoa
- 1 lime / 1 carrot
- 150 g cucumber

Preparation:

1. The quinoa needs to be prepared as per the package's directions after washing. You have to peel and chop the ginger.
2. Grate the lime zest in order to release the juice. Combine these two ingredients with the rice vinegar, ginger, oil, soy sauce, and chili sauce. Blend thoroughly.
3. After chopping the tofu, it is marinated in the sauce for five minutes. Peeling and coreing the pineapple is the first step.
4. Chop the flesh. Remove the avocado's stone to prepare it. Using the same knife, cut the avocado flesh and the cucumber. Before serving, drizzle the avocado with lime juice. Peeling the carrot beforehand will help with preparation.
5. Slice the jalapeño and roll up the chives into little bits.
6. After adding some quinoa to each bowl, garnish with cucumber, carrots, pineapple, and tofu. Cover the meat with a small amount of marinade. Before serving, add a sprinkle of chopped chives and chopped chili.

Ingredients for 3 portions:

- 200 g cooked rice
- 300 g raw tuna
- 30 ml vegetable oil
- ½ Mango
- 2.5 g wasabi paste
- ½ Avocado
- 15 g Japanese ponzu sauce
- ½ cup seaweed salad
- 1 pinch of red Hawaiian salt
- 2.5 g black sesame seeds

Preparation:

1. After cleaning, remove the tuna's skin.
2. Cut the tuna into cubes after that. Combine the wasabi paste, oil, salt, and ponzu sauce. Let the tuna marinade in the refrigerator.
3. Peel, pit, and chop the flesh from the mango and avocado in the interim.
4. Sesame seeds should be toasted in a fat-free pan. Arrange the rice into bowls, then add the avocado, mango, and tuna over top. Add the seaweed salad as a garnish. Before serving, sprinkle some sesame seeds on top.

13. Salmon and sesame poke

Ingredients for 2 portions:

- 1 packet of tortilla chips
- 250 g salmon
- ½ Lime
- 2 spring onions
- 1 garlic clove
- 45 ml soy sauce
- 1 ginger
- 30 ml sesame oil
- 5 ml sesame seeds

Preparation:

1. Toast the sesame seeds in a pan devoid of grease.
2. You should squeeze the lime. In a mixing bowl, combine the soy sauce, oil, and lime juice. Seeds from sesame are added.
3. Peel and crush the garlic cloves into the sauce. Peel and finely chop the ginger before adding it to the mixture. After washing, chop the green sections of the spring onions into rings.
4. Add both to the sauce, stirring to combine. Salmon should be cut into cubes and marinated in the sauce for a few minutes in the refrigerator.
5. Transfer to serving dishes. Lastly, top the casserole with the tortilla chips.

Ingredients for 3 portions:
- 300 ml water / 200 g sepia-colored tagliatelle
- 6 tablespoons brown sugar / 300 g salmon
- 1 handful of pecan nuts / 60 g soy sauce
- 15 g wasabi / 30 ml sesame oil
- 1 pomegranate / 15 g white sesame seeds
- 15 strawberries / 15 g black sesame seeds
- 1 mango / 200 g edamame
- 60 g mayonnaise
- ½ Ginger
- 10 g poppy seeds
- 15 g honey

Preparation:
1. Tagliatelle should be prepared in accordance with the directions on the package. Next, drain and combine with a small amount of olive oil.
2. Combine the soy sauce, sesame oil, and both black and white sesame seeds. After chopping the fish into cubes, let it sit in the marinade.
3. Cube the mango using a knife. The strawberries are ready to eat once they have been cleaned and cut. Peel the pomegranate and edamame to prepare them.
4. Mix the mayonnaise thoroughly with the honey and poppy seeds. Grate and peel the ginger. Blend it with the mayonnaise and add a small amount of water to thin the mixture. Cut the pecan nuts into small pieces.
5. In a saucepan, dissolve one hundred milliliters of water with the sugar. Next, include the pecan nuts into the mixture and let it caramelize.
6. Make an arrangement using the noodles. Drizzle with mayonnaise.

Next, arrange the fish onto the dish. Around the salmon, arrange the pomegranate, mango, edamame, and strawberries in a circle. Top with the pecan nuts. Lastly, garnish with five milliliters of wasabi.

15. Tuna with onions and macadamia nuts

Ingredients for 4 portions:

- 1 pinch of salt and pepper
- 800 g raw tuna
- 75 g macadamia nuts
- 100 g onions
- 200 ml soy sauce
- 50 g green onions
- 30 ml sesame oil

Preparation:

1. Chop and peel the onion. After washing, sprinkle salt on the tuna.
2. Chop the spring onions and combine them with the tuna and sliced onions.
3. Next, include the macadamia nuts, sesame oil, and soy sauce into the blend.
4. Add pepper to taste and store in the refrigerator to infuse.

16. Sesame tuna

Ingredients for 2 portions:
- 1 packet of pak choi
- 500 g tuna steak
- 5 ml macadamia nuts
- 50 ml soy sauce
- 5 ml sesame seeds
- 2 leeks
- 1 pinch of coarse Hawaiian salt
- 5 ml ginger
- 1 chili pepper

Preparation:
1. It's necessary to peel and chop the ginger. Cut the macadamia nuts into pieces as well. The leek needs to be cut into rings after washing.
2. The chilli pepper should be cleaned, the seeds removed, and then diced. Toast the nuts and sesame seeds in a fat-free pan.
3. Toss in the tuna and chop. After combining all the ingredients, set aside the pak choi and let the tuna absorb in the refrigerator for a minimum of two hours.
4. The pak choi should be sliced after washing. After placing the leaves on the plates, arrange the tuna on top of the leaves.

Chapter 4: Smoothie Bowls

17. Tropical smoothie bowl

- Preparation time: 20 minutes

Ingredients:

- 1 small ripe mango
- 200 g pineapple
- 2 ripe bananas
- 30 ml coconut yogurt
- 150 ml coconut milk
- 2 passion fruits, halved, pitted
- A handful of blueberries
- 30 ml coconut flakes
- a few mint leaves

Preparation:

1. Blend the yogurt, coconut milk, bananas, pineapple, and mango in a blender until smooth.
2. After dividing the mixture equally between two bowls, top with shredded coconut, blueberries, passion fruit, and mint leaves.
3. After being kept at room temperature, refrigerate for a day. Just before serving, scatter the topping over the dish.

Nutritional information:

- 330 kcal, carbohydrates: 41 g, fat: 15 g, protein: 4 g

18. Raspberry and chia pudding smoothie bowl

- Preparation time: 10 minutes

Ingredients:

- 50 g white chia seeds
- 200 ml coconut milk
- 1 nectarine
- 30 g goji berries

For the raspberry puree

- 100 g raspberries
- 5 ml lemon juice
- 10 g maple syrup

Preparation:

1. In two different bowls, thoroughly mix the coconut milk and the chia seeds. Keep the mixture on the heat for five minutes, stirring now and again, until the seeds start to swell and the consistency gets thicker.
2. In the meanwhile, combine all of the puree's ingredients in a small food processor or hand blender. After placing a spoonful in the middle of each bowl, arrange the slices of peach or nectarine, and top with goji berries. Right before serving, sprinkle the toppings over the top.

Nutritional information:

- 300 kcal, carbohydrates: 26 g, fat: 10 g, protein: 8 g

19. Rainbow smoothie bowl

- Preparation time: 20 minutes

Ingredients:

- 50 g spinach
- 1 avocado
- 1 ripe mango
- 1 Apple
- 200 ml almond milk
- 1 dragon fruit
- 100 g mixed berries (strawberries, raspberries, blueberries)

Preparation:

1. Blend the almond milk, spinach, avocado, mango, and apple in a blender until the mixture is smooth.
2. When ready to serve, divide the mixture equally between two bowls and top with the berries and dragon fruit.

Nutritional information:

- 250 kcal, carbohydrates: 19 g, fat: 16 g, protein: 4 g

- Preparation time: 5 minutes

Ingredients:
- 10 g açaí powder
- A handful of frozen berries
- ½ very ripe banana
- A handful of ice cubes
- 5 ml coconut flakes
- 5 pineapple pieces
- ½ Passion fruit
- 15 g roasted rolled oats

Preparation:
3. Blend together 100 cc of water, acai powder, frozen berries, banana, and ice cubes in a high-powered blender. Process till smooth.
4. After blending all the ingredients until well combined, transfer the mixture to a bowl and garnish with desired ingredients.

Nutritional information:
- 180 kcal, carbohydrates: 19 g, fat: 8 g, protein: 3 g

21. Turmeric smoothie bowl

- Preparation time: 10 minutes

Ingredients:

- 10 g ground turmeric
- 45 g coconut milk yogurt
- 50 g gluten-free rolled oats
- 15 g cashew nut butter
- 2 bananas
- 2.5 g ground cinnamon
- 15 g chia seeds or chopped nuts to serve

Preparation:

1. In a blender, combine all the ingredients together with the 600 milliliters of water; process until smooth. To serve, transfer into a bowl and top with chopped almonds or chia seeds.

Nutritional information:

- 290 kcal, carbohydrates: 40 g, fat: 10 g, protein: 7 g

- Preparation time: 5 minutes

Ingredients:
- 500 ml carrot juice
- 200 g pineapple
- 2 bananas
- small piece of ginger
- 20 g cashew nuts
- Juice of one lime

Preparation:
1. In a blender, combine all the ingredients and process until fully smooth. You have two options: pour it into a dish or consume it right now. After storing, place in the refrigerator for a day.

Nutritional information:
- 170 kcal, carbohydrates: 30 g, fat: 4 g, protein: 3 g

23. Breakfast shake bowl

- Preparation time: 5 minutes

Ingredients:
- 100 ml whole milk
- 30 ml. Natural yoghurt
- 1 banana
- 150 g frozen wild berries
- 50 g blueberries
- 15 g chia seeds
- 2.5 g cinnamon
- 15 g goji berries
- 5 ml mixed seeds
- 5 ml honey

Preparation:
1. In a blender, combine all the ingredients and process until fully smooth. Transfer into a glass, relax, and savor!

Nutritional information:
- 390 kcal, carbohydrates: 50 g, fat: 12 g, protein: 15 g

- Preparation time: 5 minutes

Ingredients:

- 160 g ripe strawberries
- 160 g baby spinach
- 1 small avocado
- 150 ml organicyogurt
- 2 small oranges

Preparation:

1. In a blender, combine all the ingredients and process until fully smooth. Once the required consistency is achieved, thoroughly stir in a few drops of cold water. Transfer to a bowl and start eating right away.

Nutritional information:

- 225 kcal, carbohydrates: 16 g, fat: 13 g, protein: 8 g

- Preparation time: 5 minutes

Ingredients:

- 3 peeled kiwis
- 1 mango
- 500 ml pineapple juice
- 1 banana

Preparation:

1. After adding all the ingredients to a blender and blending until smooth, transfer the mixture into a bowl.

Nutritional information:

- 160 kcal, carbohydrates: 36 g, fat: 1 g, protein: 2 g

- Preparation time: 5 minutes

Ingredients:

- 1 Orange
- 1 large carrot
- 2 stalks of celery
- 50 g mango, roughly chopped
- 200 ml water

Preparation:

Put the orange, carrot, celery, and peeled mango into a blender; add the remaining water to the container and process until the mixture is smooth.

Once in the bowl, pour and serve.

Nutritional information:

- 120 kcal, carbohydrates: 25 g, fat: 1 g, protein: 3 g

27. Muesli smoothie bowl

- Preparation time: 5 minutes

Ingredients:

- 1 large banana
- 75 g cooked beet
- 175 g strawberries
- 2 kiwis
- 1 medium-sized mango
- 75 g blueberries
- 50 g raspberries
- 1 fig
- 60 g blackberries
- 20 g muesli
- 1 Orange
- 60 g strawberries
- 20 g chia seeds

Preparation:

1. In a blender or food processor, combine all the ingredients except the garnishes; blend or process until the desired consistency is reached.
2. Transfer to two different bowls.
3. Lastly, group these elements in close proximity to one another: granola, strawberries, oranges, blackberries, figs, and chia seeds.

Nutritional information:

- 290 kcal, carbohydrates: 63 g, fat: 3 g, protein: 5 g

- Preparation time: 10 minutes

Ingredients:

- 350 g frozen raspberries
- 3 tablespoons natural yogurt
- 5 ml vanilla pod pulp (optional)
- 300 ml freshly squeezed orange juice
- 15 g honey
- 80 g pomegranate seeds in a saucepan
- 6 clementines
- 30 ml chia seeds (optional)

Preparation:

1. Blend the raspberries, yogurt, vanilla extract (if using), orange juice, honey and most of the pomegranate seeds in a blender until frothy.
2. Divide the mixture evenly between four shallow bowls. Drizzle over a little yogurt if desired and sprinkle with the clementines, the rest of the pomegranate and some chia seeds.

Nutritional information:

- 111 kcal, carbohydrates: 24 g, fat: 1 g, protein: 3 g

29. Smoothie bowl with lime and mango

- Preparation time: 10 minutes

Ingredients:

- 1 ripe, juicy pear
- 1 ripe banana
- 30 g porridge
- 15 g clear honey
- 110 g low-fat natural yogurt
- 250 ml apple juice
- A handful of ice cubes

Preparation:

1. Mix all the ingredients in a blender until very smooth.
2. To present, split the soup into two bowls and top each with a couple of fresh mint sprigs and a slice of lime.

Nutritional information:

- 90 kcal, carbohydrates: 14 g, fat: 2 g, protein: 3 g

30. Fruity yogurt smoothie bowl

- Preparation time: 20 minutes

Ingredients:
- 1 small banana, peeled and chopped
- 450 g raspberries
- 400 ml skimmed milk
- 200 ml low-fat yogurt
- 75 ml honey

Preparation:
1. In a food processor, combine all the ingredients and pulse until smooth. To achieve a more uniform texture, strain the raspberry mixture to eliminate any seeds using a sieve.
2. Transfer half to two different bowls. Garnish each with a couple of whole raspberries.

Nutritional information:
- 136 kcal, carbohydrates: 25 g, fat: 1 g, protein: 7 g

31. Breakfast bowl with pear, banana, oats and honey

- Preparation time: 20 minutes

Ingredients:
- 1 ripe, juicy pear
- 1 ripe banana

- 30 ml porridge
- 15 g clear honey
- 110 g low-fat natural yogurt
- 250 ml apple juice
- A handful of ice cubes

Preparation:

1. In a food processor, combine all the ingredients and process until a smooth consistency is reached.
2. In the bowl, serve the food cold.

Nutritional information:

- 250 kcal, carbohydrates: 50 g, fat: 2 g, protein: 5 g

Chapter 5: Buddha Bowls

32. Chicken with quinoa

Ingredients for 2 portions:
- Sesame seeds / 2 chicken breast fillets
- ½ spring onion / 1 avocado
- ¼ red bell pepper / 150 g red quinoa
- 4 broccoli florets / 3 cherry tomatoes
- 1 zucchini / 6 mushrooms
- 100 g rocket
- For the dressing:
- Salt and pepper / 100 g yogurt
- 5 ml olive oil / 5 ml soy sauce

Preparation:
1. Slice the zucchinis into rounds after washing. After removing the skin and seeds from the peppers, chop the flesh into small pieces. Slice the spring onion lengthwise.
2. As directed on the package, prepare the quinoa according to the directions. Season the meat with salt and pepper after frying it in a pan with a small amount of oil on all sides.
3. For a few minutes, sauté the mushrooms together with the remaining vegetables. Combine all of the dressing's components. After removing the avocado's stone, thinly slice the flesh.
4. Slice the chicken into thin pieces. After washing, serve the rocket. Scatter the quinoa over it.
5. Arrange the vegetables and meat in their proper locations. Drizzle with the dressing and top with the toasted sesame seeds.

33. Couscous with feta and radishes

Ingredients for 2 portions:
- 70 g feta / 10 quail eggs
- 100 g rocket / 150 g couscous

- 6 cocktail tomatoes / 6 radishes
- 1 avocado / 2 stalks of celery
- For the dressing:
- 1 pinch of pepper / 2 tablespoons of olive oil
- 5 ml salt
- 45 g balsamic vinegar
- Juice 1 lemon

Preparation:

1. Boil the quail eggs for three minutes to prepare them. Follow the instructions while preparing the couscous.
2. Slice the avocado's flesh thinly after removing the stone. Slice the celery and radishes thinly after cleaning. Halve the tomatoes. The rocket ship has to be cleaned.
3. Combine all the ingredients to make the dressing. Time to serve the rocket. Top the couscous with the vegetables, then finish with the eggs.
4. The salad should be dressed with the dressing and garnished with the feta.

34. Quinoa with sweet potatoes and vegetables

Ingredients for 2 portions:

- ½ avocado / 150 g red quinoa
- 4 cocktail tomatoes / 100 g lettuce
- 1 zucchini / edamame
- For the sweet potato:
- 3 cloves / 1 sweet potato

For the dressing:

- 1 pinch of pepper / 60 g tahini
- 1.5 g salt / 2.5 g soy sauce
- A little olive oil.

Preparation:

1. For thirty minutes, bring the sweet potatoes and cloves to a boil in water. Follow the directions to prepare the quinoa.
2. Slice the zucchini thinly and split the tomatoes in half. After removing the avocado's stone, thinly slice the flesh.
3. Heat up a pan with a little oil first. Add salt and pepper and fry the edamame, tomatoes, and zucchini in the oil.
4. Combine all the ingredients to make the dressing. Spoon the salad into dishes to serve. Place the sweet potato, quinoa, and veggies over top. Sprinkle some toasted sesame seeds on top and drizzle with a little dressing.

35.   Mediterranean Buddha bowl

Ingredients for 2 portions:

- 20 cocktail tomatoes
- 100 g alphabet grain
- 1 green chili pepper
- 100 g mixed lettuce
- 80 g white beans
- 100 g turkey meat

Preparation:

1. Cut the used turkey into dice. Make sure you follow the directions when preparing the savory cereal.
2. Add salt, pepper, and tomato purée to the meat to season it properly. Next, cook it in a pan. Chop the tomatoes lengthwise. Sieve the beans, please. Cut the peppers into rings to prepare them.
3. Use water to give the lettuce a wash. In a bowl, stir together the lemon juice, olive oil, salt, and pepper. Include the olive oil. Arrange the salad.
4. Arrange the plate with the meat and bean cake. Arrange the vegetables in a uniform layer on top. Before serving, the dish should be covered with the dressing.

36. Buckwheat noodles with salmon and vegetables

Ingredients for 2 portions:

- Black sesame seeds
- 4 broccoli florets / 150 g buckwheat noodles
- 1 handful of edamame / 1 zucchini
- 6 mangetout / 1 bell bell pepper
- Red cabbage / 4 cocktail tomatoes
- 6 Mushrooms
- For the salmon:
- 1 salmon fillet / salt and pepper
- 15 g sweet chili sauce
- For the dressing:
- Salt and pepper / 60 g hummus
- 2.5 g sesame oil / 2.5 g apple cider vinegar

Preparation:

1. Slice the red cabbage into thin strips. Make quarters out of the mushrooms. Using a knife, remove the seeds and skin off the peppers and chop them into cubes. Clean and cut the zucchini.
2. Before draining, let the noodles boil in salted water for three minutes. In a skillet with a little oil, sauté the mushrooms, mangetout, edamame, broccoli, tomatoes, and zucchini. Add salt and pepper to taste the entire meal.
3. Before frying, season the salmon with salt, pepper, and chili sauce in a separate pan with a little oil.
4. Combine all of the dressing's components. After washing, proceed to serve the salad. The salmon should be layered over everything. Add the pasta and vegetables to the salmon, covering it completely. Drizzle with part of the dressing and top with toasted sesame seeds right before serving.

37. Pumpkin with spinach and quinoa

Ingredients for 2 portions:

- 150 g quinoa
- 200 g Hokkaido pumpkin / 1 avocado
- 100 g lamb's lettuce / 100 g baby spinach
- For the dressing:
- Salt and pepper / 45 g walnut oil
- 30 ml apple cider vinegar
- To garnish:
- 1 handful of raisins
- 1 handful of walnut kernels

Preparation:

1. Dice the pumpkin flesh after peeling it. Add salt, pepper, and olive oil to food that is going to be roasted in the oven.
2. After that, add the pumpkin and bake at 180 degrees Celsius for 20 minutes. Follow the instructions to prepare the quinoa. Slice the avocado's flesh into thin strips after removing the stone.
3. Presentable salad presentation is key. Add the pumpkin, avocado, spinach, and quinoa on top. Combine the dressing's contents in a bowl and drizzle over the salad. As a garnish, include some chopped raisins and walnuts.

38. Tofu with red cabbage and wild rice

Ingredients for 2 portions:

- 100 g wild rice
- 100 g mixed salad / 3 mushrooms
- Red cabbage / bell bell pepper
- 60 g chickpeas from the tin
- Black sesame seeds
- For the tofu:
- 5 ml black sesame seeds / 4 smoked tofu
- 15 g teriyaki sauce
- For the dressing:
- Salt and pepper / 45 g honey
- 30 ml soy sauce

Preparation:

1. Follow the directions on the package to prepare the rice. Cube the tofu with a knife.
2. In a skillet with a little hot oil, fry the tofu. Combine the sesame seeds and teriyaki sauce, then use it to season the tofu. After cleaning, cut the mushrooms into quarters.
3. Chop the red cabbage into bite-sized pieces. Cut the peppers into small pieces after removing the seeds and skin. In a skillet, fry the mushrooms. Sort the chickpeas using a strainer.
4. Combine all of the dressing's components. Place the veggies, rice, and tofu on top of the salad. Drizzle everything with the dressing, then top with sesame seeds.

39. Beans and olives with sweet potatoes

Ingredients for 2 portions:

- 1 handful of walnut kernels
- 150 g kidney beans / 12 olives
- 100 g mixed lettuce
- 1 sweet potato / 1 turnip
- 150 g quinoa / 10 broccoli florets
- 1 red bell bell pepper
- For the dressing:
- 45 g soy sauce / 45 g sesame oil

Preparation:

1. Follow the instructions to prepare the quinoa. Slice the peppers lengthwise into thin strips after removing the seeds and skin. Peel and cut the sweet potato into cubes to prepare it.
2. Using a knife, thinly slice the beet. Peel and chop the cucumber into cubes to start preparing it. Empty the beans. Get the potatoes ready to eat.
3. Heat up a pan with a little oil first. Combine the broccoli and peppers in a pan and add a little salt to taste.
4. Combine all the ingredients for the dressing and add salt and pepper to taste. It is necessary to wash and serve the salad.
5. Arrange the beans, quinoa, olives, and vegetables over top. After that, drizzle the dressing on top and garnish with the walnuts.

40. Tofu with chicory and mushrooms

Ingredients for 1 portion:

- 15 g black sesame seeds
- 1 portion of udon noodles
- Soy sauce
- 200 g smoked tofu
- Smoked salt
- 1 handful of oyster mushrooms
- Agave syrup
- 1 bell bell pepper
- 1 handful of steamed cabbage sprouts
- 1 chicory

Preparation:

1. First, get the noodles ready. After cutting the tofu into cubes, fry it in oil. After removing the peppers' seeds and peel, chop them into bite-sized pieces.
2. Add the oyster mushrooms and peppers to the tofu and fry it all together. Before frying, the chicory needs to be chopped into strips.
3. Add to the shredded Brussels sprouts. To prepare the dressing, combine the soy sauce, smoked salt, and agave syrup.
4. Place all the ingredients in the specified order on the plate, and then top with the toasted sesame seeds and dressing.

41. Beef with vegetables

Ingredients for 4 portions:

- 1 zucchini
- 400-500 g beef / cress
- Peanut oil / 1 bunch of Thai basil
- 200 g short grain rice / radish
- 100-150 g cherry tomatoes
- For the marinade:
- Sesame seeds / 15 g dark soy sauce
- 1 spring onion / 15 g oyster sauce
- 5 ml rice wine vinegar / 5 ml ginger
- 5 ml honey / 2.5 g garlic
- 5 ml sesame oil / 1 red chili pepper

Preparation:

1. Wash and cut the cherry tomatoes into quarters. Slice the radish very thinly. Slice the zucchinis into rounds after washing. Finely grated the ginger. Peel and grate the garlic to prepare it.
2. Take out and discard the chili pepper's seeds. Cube the meat, if necessary. The pan's oil is heated. In the pan, brown the meat. After all of the marinade ingredients have been well combined, let the meat sit for ten to fifteen minutes.
3. After adding the rice, give the container a little tap. Cover the meat with a small amount of marinade. After that, arrange the zucchini, tomatoes, radishes, and sliced pork on top. Lastly, add some spring onions, basil, and cress.

Ingredients for 3 portions:

- For the chickpeas:
- Salt / 400 g canned chickpeas
- 1.5 g paprika powder / olive oil
- 1.5 g cayenne pepper / 1.5 g garam masala
- For the pasta:
- 1.5 g pepper / 230 g soba noodles
- 15 g lemon juice / 15 g sesame oil
- 1.5 g salt

For the hummus:

- Salt and pepper / 100 g tinned chickpeas
- 5 ml baking powder / olive oil
- ½ clove of garlic / 30 ml cold water
- 2.5 g cumin / 30 ml lemon juice
- 5 ml tahini paste
- For the vegetables:
- 80 g Chinese cabbage / 1 broccoli
- 80 g red bell pepper / 180 g kale
- 80 g pickled artichokes / 1 pinch of salt
- 100 g tomatoes / 2 carrots

Preparation:

1. First, set the oven temperature to 175 degrees Celsius. Rinse and strain 400 grams of chickpeas. Next, roll the chickpeas to extract the skin and make it looser. After that, let the chickpeas dry.

2. Arrange a baking pan with the chickpeas, olive oil, and spices. Transfer the tray to the oven and bake for forty minutes. Every now and again, turn.

3. Noodles should be cooked as directed on the package. Next, combine with the spices, sesame oil, and the juice from half a lemon. Combine all of the hummus's components and then add salt and pepper to

taste. after washing and chopping the broccoli into florets.

4. Rinse the broccoli florets after blanching them for three to four minutes in salted water. With a vegetable peeler, cut the peppers, Chinese cabbage, and red cabbage into strips.

5. Add the kale, lemon juice, and a small pinch of salt and mix everything together. After peeling, thinly slice the carrots. Halve the tomatoes. Arrange the veggies, pasta, and chickpeas in the desired order. Finally, top with a dab of hummus.

43.   Shirtake noodles with sesame dressing:

Ingredients for 2 portions:

- 30 ml sesame seeds
- 150 g shirtake noodles
- 100 g edamame
- ½ Cucumber
- 100 g mixed salad
- ½ Courgette
- 3 carrots
- For the dressing:
- 45 g soy sauce
- 60 g sesame oil

Preparation:

1. Pasta should be prepared as directed per the recipe. Chop the cucumber into bite-sized pieces.
2. Slice the zucchinis into thin strips. After pealing, grate the carrots. Heat up a pan with a little oil first. Fry the zucchinis in it to prepare them. Combine all of the dressing's components. Organize the salad so that it looks good.
3. Arrange the noodles and veggies on top. After adding the dressing, toss everything together.

44. Green Buddha bowl

Ingredients for 1 portion:
- Coriander
- 1 avocado
- Salt and pepper
- ¼ Broccoli head
- 30 ml olive oil
- 250 g canned chickpeas
- 30 ml vinegar
- 1 handful of spinach leaves
- 15 g fresh herbs of your choice

Preparation:
1. Steam the broccoli first. Once the chickpeas are drained, you should pan-cook them. Stir the chickpeas after adding some salt, pepper, and ground coriander.
2. Oil and vinegar are the components of the salad dressing. Cut the avocado flesh into wedges after removing the stone.
3. Arrange the salad around the outside of the serving bowl in a circle. After adding the avocado, broccoli, and chickpeas, season with salt, pepper, and other herbs.

45. Sweet potatoes with chickpeas

Ingredients for 3 portions:

For the bowl:

- Salt and pepper / 1 sweet potato
- 30 ml olive oil / 100 g quinoa
- 2.5 g cinnamon / 400 g canned chickpeas
- 150 g kale
- For the dressing:
- Salt/olive oil
- Juice of 1 lime / 45 g almond butter
- 15 g soy sauce / 30 ml tahini
- 15 g maple syrup

Preparation:

1. Set the oven's temperature to 200 degrees Celsius first. Peel and cut into cubes the potatoes to prepare them. Add the olive oil, cinnamon, salt, pepper, and chili powder to the potatoes in a baking dish.
2. After putting everything in the oven, bake for thirty minutes. Rinse the quinoa under running water and cook as directed on the package.
3. Take the kale leaves off after washing. After that, cook the kale for two to four minutes in salted water.
4. Combine all the ingredients for the dressing and add salt and pepper to taste. Use water to rinse the chickpeas. Arrange the potatoes, quinoa, chickpeas, and greens on a platter. After that, pour the dressing over them.

46. Sweet potatoes with egg

Ingredients for 2 portions:

- 50 g pistachios / 2 sweet potatoes
- 4 handfuls of spinach leaves / 10 g turmeric
- 120 g brown rice / 2 garlic cloves
- 4 eggs / 480 ml vegetable stock
- 15 g olive oil

For the dressing:

- 1.5 g salt
- 60 ml lemon juice
- 4 sprigs of parsley
- 80 ml olive oil
- 15 g maple syrup

Preparation:

1. Peel, cut, and wash the potatoes to prepare them. In a pan, bring the olive oil to a boil. Put the potatoes in it to steam.
2. Garlic should be peeled before being chopped. Before adding the garlic, combine the potatoes with the turmeric.
3. Deglaze the pan with the veggie stock and let everything simmer. Next, purée. After washing, place the rice in three times its original volume of water and bring to a boil.
4. After that, simmer it over low heat for twenty minutes. Heat the water in the sous vide burner until it reaches a temperature of 75°C. Crack the eggs into individual bowls and set aside to rest for 15 minutes in the sous vide cooker.
5. Chop the parsley and combine it with the other ingredients to make the dressing. Together with the rice, eggs, and spinach, serve the mashed potatoes. Drizzle with the dressing and garnish with a handful of pistachios.

47. Colorful Buddha bowl with tofu

Ingredients for 2 portions:

- For the bowl:
- 5 ml sesame seeds
- 3 handfuls of mixed salad
- 15 g olive oil / 2 carrots
- 200 g tofu / 1 handful of radishes
- 3 mushrooms / 1 handful of bean sprouts
- 200 g chickpeas / 1 handful red cabbage
- ½ avocado / 1 red pointed bell pepper
- For the dressing:
- Salt and pepper
- 45 g tahini / 15 g olive oil / juice of 1 lemon

Preparation:

1. Cut the veggies and salad into bite-sized pieces after washing. Warm up the frying pan's oil.
2. Fry the tofu until it turns golden brown on both sides. Combine all of the dressing's components. Organize the salad so that it looks good. Put the tofu and veggies in order. Once the dressing has been added, serve.

Chapter 6: Protein-Rich Bowls

48. Cod with spinach skin

- Preparation time: 27 minutes

Ingredients:
- 100 g wholegrain spaghetti
- 1 large onion
- 15 g rapeseed oil
- 1 red chili pepper, deseeded and sliced
- 2 cloves of garlic, chopped
- 200 g cherry tomatoes, halved
- 5 ml apple cider vinegar
- 10 g capers
- 5 olives, halved
- 2.5 g smoked paprika
- 2 cod fillets
- 160 g spinach leaves
- a small handful of chopped parsley

Preparation:
1. Add the spinach to the spaghetti for the final two minutes of cooking after the ten minutes have passed.
2. In the meantime, cook the onion in a big, nonstick frying pan with oil until it turns golden brown. After adding the tomatoes to the pan, stir in the garlic and chili powder.
3. Pour in the vinegar and stir in the olives, capers, and peppers. For a further five to seven minutes, fry the cod fillets on the pan with a lid on.
4. After draining, arrange the pasta and spinach in bowls, then add the fish and sauce on top. Before serving, add a little chopped parsley on top.

Nutritional information:
- 440 kcal, carbohydrates: 45 g, fat: 10 g, protein: 35 g

- Preparation time: 20 minutes

Ingredients:
- 250 g wholegrain rice
- 30 ml. chopped ginger
- 4 spring onions
- 160 g broccoli
- 225 g lean fillet steak

Preparation:
1. Transfer the rice mixture to a bowl and stir in the ginger, water, and chopped onions.
2. Add the broccoli and white spring onions; reserve the onions for the top because you'll need them for the following stage. Place in the microwave and cook, covered, for five minutes.
3. In a nonstick skillet that has been warmed, fry the steak for two minutes on each side.
4. After that, put aside. Take out the onion whites from the bowl and add them to the pan with the steak while it's resting, allowing them to brown a little bit in the meat juices.
5. Split the mixture of rice between two sizable plates. After slicing the steak, place the sautéed onions on it.

Nutritional information:
- 380 kcal, carbohydrates: 38 g, fat: 10 g, protein: 30 g

50. Bowl with salad and grilled halloumi

- Preparation time: 30 minutes

Ingredients

- 45 g olive oil
- 1 small red onion, sliced
- 1 large roasted bell pepper
- 200 g quinoa
- 500 ml vegetable stock
- small bunch of flat-leaf parsley, roughly chopped
- Zest and juice of 1 lemon
- large pinch of sugar
- 250 g halloumicheese, cut into 6 slices

Preparation:

1. Put hot oil in a medium saucepan (15 g). Cook the onion and bell pepper for a few minutes, then add the quinoa and heat for an additional three minutes.
2. Splash in the stock, cover, and simmer. Cook for 15 minutes, then stir in half of the parsley.
3. Meanwhile, combine the remaining parsley, oil, lemon zest, and juice with a good teaspoon of salt and sugar.
4. The halloumi should be crispy and golden brown after frying on both sides. After serving the salad, drizzle the dressing over the halloumi.

Nutritional information:

- 600 kcal, carbohydrates: 40 g, fat: 37 g, protein: 33 g

51. Indian chicken protein bowl

- Preparation time: 10 minutes

Ingredients:
- 90 g lentils with Indian spice
- 160 g cherry tomatoes
- 150 g cooked chicken meat without skin
- A handful of fresh coriander, chopped
- 60 g tzatziki

Preparation:
1. Tear a corner off the lentil packet and give it a minute in the microwave. After allowing it to cool, split between two enormous basins.
2. Serve with tzatziki and garnish with the chicken and cherry tomatoes. Garnish with fresh coriander.

Nutritional information:
- 230 kcal, carbohydrates: 12 g, fat: 7 g, protein: 30 g

52. Salad bowl with turkey and pomegranate

- Preparation time: 40 minutes

Ingredients

- 2 tablespoons each of chopped dill, parsley and mint
- Zest and juice of 1 lemon
- 15 g harissa paste
- 500 g turkey
- 30 ml white wine or water
- 250 g bulgur wheat or a mixture
- 2 tomatoes
- ½ Cucumber, diced
- 100 g pomegranate seeds

Preparation:

1. Set oven temperature to 200°C. Combine half of the herbs, half of the harissa with a hint of spice, and half of the lemon juice and zest. After rubbing the turkey with the marinade, let it sit for five minutes.
2. Unfold a sizable section of foil. Cover with the turkey, marinade, wine, or water, then seal the foil by folding the edges together. Put another foil layer on top. After putting the parcel on a baking tray, bake it for 30 minutes, or until it's done.
3. While waiting, put the salad together. Follow the directions on the package to cook the bulgur. After draining, combine with pomegranate seeds, tomatoes, cucumber, lemon juice, and zest. Cut the turkey into slices, place it over the salad, and drizzle it with the foil's juice.

Nutritional information:

- 300 kcal, carbohydrates: 23 g, fat: 7 g, protein: 41 g

53. Bowl with Cobb and buttermilk dressing

- Preparation time: 15 minutes

Ingredients

- Lettuce leaves
- 1 avocado
- 2 plum tomatoes
- 3 slices of cooked crispy bacon
- 140 g cooked turkey breast or chicken, cut into bite-sized pieces
- 2 hard-boiled eggs, chopped into pieces

For the dressing

- 75 ml buttermilk
- 30 ml light mayonnaise
- 15 g. White wine vinegar
- 15 g chopped dill
- ½ clove of garlic, crushed

Preparation:

1. In a small dish, combine the dressing ingredients with a dash of salt. After tossing the salad with the dressing, divide the ingredients into bowls.

Nutritional information:

- 470 kcal, carbohydrates: 8 g, fat: 30 g, protein: 43 g

- Preparation time: 50 minutes

Ingredients

- 15 g olive oil
- 1 onion
- 2 red peppers
- 45 g tomato puree
- 400 g tins of chopped tomatoes
- 4 skinless chicken breasts
- 140 g quinoa
- 2 cubes chicken stock
- 400 g pinto beans, drained
- small bunch of coriander
- Juice of 1 lime
- 15 g sugar
- Natural yogurt to serve

Preparation:

1. Fry the peppers and onions for a few minutes until they become tender in a deep pan filled with hot oil. Stir in the tomatoes and tomato purée after a minute. Cover with water and simmer moderately. Add the chicken breast and simmer it gently for 20 minutes after the chicken is fully cooked.

2. After adding the stock cubes, heat up a large pan of water until it boils. When the quinoa is cooked, add it and simmer for 15 minutes. Last minute, add the beans. After completely drained, mix in the coriander and lime juice.

3. Transfer the chicken to a cutting board and use a fork to shred each breast. Stir the tomato sauce after adding the sugar and spices once more. Accompany the quinoa with a dollop of yogurt, sprinkle some coriander leaves on top, and savor.

Nutritional information:

- 330 kcal, carbohydrates: 34 g, fat: 6 g, protein: 33 g

55. Bowl with turkey meat and clementines

- Preparation time: 30 minutes

Ingredients

- 1 red onion, halved and thinly sliced
- 1 lemon
- 300 g diced turkey breast
- 30 ml rapeseed oil
- 2 clementines
- 2 cloves of garlic, chopped
- 400 g green lentils, drained
- 15 g balsamic vinegar
- 1 bell bell pepper, quartered and sliced
- a small handful of mint
- 4 walnut halves

Preparation:

1. In a bowl, combine the onion and lemon juice. Put the turkey, garlic, lemon zest, and half of the oil in a bowl. Then give it a good stir.
2. Transfer the lentils to two bowls and add the balsamic vinegar. In a big nonstick wok, heat the remaining oil. Add the peppers and sauté for 3 minutes.
3. Add the turkey meat and half of the onion and continue to sauté until the peppers are tender and the meat is cooked through. Combine the lentils with the clementine flesh, remaining onion, mint, and walnut bits.

Nutritional information:

- 500 kcal, carbohydrates: 34 g, fat: 18 g, protein: 48 g

56. Bowl with wild salmon and vegetables

- Preparation time: 10 minutes

Ingredients

- 2 carrots
- 1 large zucchini

- 2 cooked beet
- 30 ml balsamic vinegar
- ⅓ Small packet of dill
- 1 small red onion, finely chopped
- 280 g wild salmon
- 30 ml capers in vinegar, rinsed

Preparation:

1. Using a spiral cutter or julienne peeler, cut the carrots and zucchini into long, spaghetti-like strands and divide them between two bowls.
2. In a small bowl, combine the beet, red onion, balsamic vinegar, and chopped dill. Over the vegetables, pour the mixture. Sprinkle with the capers and more dill, if using, after adding the salmon pieces.

Nutritional information:

- 400 kcal, carbohydrates: 18 g, fat: 17 g, protein: 38 g

- Preparation time: 20 minutes

Ingredients

- 2 large eggs
- 75 g wholemeal penne
- 160 g broccoli
- 160 g fine beans, cut and halved
- 15 g miso
- 5 ml grated ginger
- 15 g rapeseed oil
- 30 ml. Sunflower seeds

Preparation:

1. After boiling the eggs vigorously for eight minutes, peel and chop them in half. Meanwhile, cook the pasta for 5 minutes, add the broccoli and beans, and continue cooking for an additional 5 minutes, or until everything is tender.
2. Once the water has been drained, combine the noodles, veggies, miso, ginger, and oil in a bowl along with 60 g of the noodle water. As a garnish, add the eggs and seeds.

Nutritional information:

- 430 kcal, carbohydrates: 31 g, fat: 22 g, protein: 25 g

- Preparation time: 25 minutes

Ingredients

- 1 eggplant
- 30 ml. Flour
- 37.5 ml olive oil
- 1 sirloin steak
- 100 g lamb's lettuce
- 50 g feta

For the dressing

- 1 green chili pepper, halved and diced
- ½ Lemon
- ½ small packet of coriander plus additional leaves for serving
- ½ small packet of mint

Preparation:

1. Season the eggplant slices with salt and flour. In a large frying pan, heat two teaspoons of olive oil until glossy. Put the eggplants in the pan and fry them for a few minutes on each side. After that, put aside. The steak should be seared for two minutes on each side after seasoning and adding it to the pan. Slice it once it has sat for five minutes.
2. Whisk together the remaining olive oil, dressing ingredients, and a tiny bit of water in a blender or small food processor. To serve, combine half of the dressing in a bowl with the lamb's lettuce. Place the crispy eggplant and steak on top. Drizzle with the remaining dressing after adding the feta. After adding the final herbs, serve.

Nutritional information:

- 450 kcal, carbohydrates: 20 g, fat: 30 g, protein: 25 g

59. Bowl with mint chicken and peach

- Preparation time: 25 minutes

Ingredients

- 1 Lime
- 15 g rapeseed oil
- 30 ml. Mint
- 1 clove of garlic, finely grated
- 2 skinless chicken breast fillets (300 g)
- 160 g fine beans
- 2 peaches (200 g)
- 1 red onion
- 165g vegetable salad
- 1 small avocado
- 240 g cooked new potatoes

Preparation:

1. Combine the garlic, oil, mint, and half of the lime zest and juice in a bowl. Thinly slice the chicken, then add it to the garlic mixture and generously season with black pepper.
2. Boil the beans in a pan of water for three to four minutes, or until they are just tender. Grill the chicken and onion for a few minutes on each side while you wait. After transferring to a dish, sauté the peaches right away.
3. Combine the onions and warmed beans with the leftover mint mixture, then serve in bowls beside the salad. After adding the mint, place the avocado, peaches, and chicken on top. Alongside the entrée, serve the potatoes.

Nutritional information:

- 500 kcal, carbohydrates: 36 g, fat: 18 g, protein: 44 g

60. Bowl with beans and meat

- Preparation time: 15 minutes

Ingredients

- 250 g dried black beans
- 100 g smoked bacon, cut into slices
- 500 g pork ribs
- 3 chorizosausages
- 500 g pork
- 3 onions
- 4 cloves of garlic, finely chopped
- A pinch of chili flakes
- Olive oil
- 2 bay leaves
- 30 ml. White wine vinegar
- steamed rice
- chopped parsley or coriander

Preparation:

1. Warm up a sizable, heavy dish that has a cover. Add the bacon and cook it till it crisps up.
2. Take out and set aside the pan's oil. Brown the pork, ribs, and sausages. To season, add salt and pepper.
3. Take out and set aside the meat. To the pan, add the onion, garlic, and chile. If needed, drizzle with a little olive oil. Add salt and

pepper for seasoning, then cook for eight minutes.

4. Add the pork, bay leaves, white wine vinegar, and drained beans.
5. Add roughly 650 milliliters of water to the surface. After it boils, lower the heat. Cook, covered, for two hours.
6. Accompany with rice, sliced oranges, paprika sauce, and a dash of coriander or parsley.

Nutritional information:

- 700 kcal, carbohydrates: 40 g, fat: 30 g, protein: 60 g

- Preparation time: 35 minutes

Ingredients

- 4 sausages
- 4 slices of bacon, diced
- 200 g mushrooms
- 350 g pasta
- 50 g Parmesan cheese
- 2 egg yolks
- bunch of parsley
- finely chopped
- 30 ml semi-fat crème fraîche

Preparation:

1. In a nonstick skillet, cook the sausage meat for 8 to 10 minutes, or until golden brown. Using a wooden spoon, loosen, take out, and place aside. Return the sausage meat and keep warm after frying for 5 to 8 minutes, or until the bacon and mushrooms are golden brown.

2. Cooking the pasta should be done as directed on the package. Combine the crème fraîche, egg yolk, parsley, and Parmesan cheese to make the sauce. Rinse the cooked pasta and transfer the cooking water to a ladle.

3. Combine the pasta and meat over a low heat and toss in the sauce. Stir rapidly after adding seasoning. Incorporate a small amount of water. Transfer to bowls and sprinkle with the remaining Parmesan and parsley.

Nutritional information:

- 700 kcal, carbohydrates: 72 g, fat: 30 g, protein: 30 g

62. High-protein pasta salad bowl

- Preparation time: 25 minutes

Ingredients

- 400 g pasta
- 4-5 tablespoons of fresh pesto
- 15 g mayonnaise
- 30 ml. Greek yogurt
- ½ Lemon
- 200 g mixed, cooked vegetables such as peas, green beans, zucchinis
- 100 g cherry tomatoes, quartered
- 200 g cooked chicken
- Ham, prawns, hard-boiled egg or cheese

Preparation:

1. Pasta should be cooked until al dente (about 11 minutes). But be careful to adhere to the directions on the container. After draining, put in a bowl. After adding the pesto, let it cool.
2. To the cooled spaghetti, add the veggies, yogurt, mayo, and lemon juice. Transfer to bowls, then sprinkle cooked chicken on top.

Nutritional information:

- 520 kcal, carbohydrates: 70 g, fat: 16 g, protein: 25 g

63. Bowl of chicken salad and bacon

- Preparation time: 45 minutes

Ingredients

- Meat from 1 roast chicken
- 6 strips of bacon
- 1 small red onion, halved, cut into thin slices
- 30 ml olive oil
- 10 g white wine vinegar
- 100 g packet of watercress
- ¾ Cucumber

For the dressing

- 200 g Greek yogurt
- 60 g mayonnaise
- 10 g wholegrain mustard
- 1 spring onion
- 10 g chopped tarragon

Preparation:

1. Season the ingredients of the dressing lightly. If needed, use a little water to soften up the chicken before adding it.
2. In a big skillet, slowly cook the bacon until it's crispy and the fat is rendered. Meanwhile, combine the onion with the oil, vinegar, and spices.
3. In a bowl, combine the watercress, cucumber, and onion. Pour some over the chicken and top with bacon. Accompany with a crusty bread.

Nutritional information:

- 500 kcal, carbohydrates: 4 g, fat: 35 g, protein: 44 g

Chapter 7: Vegan Bowls

64. Tofu and celery bowl

Ingredients for 2 portions:

- 100 g wholegrain rice
- Salt, chili powder
- 2 spring onions
- 1 stalk of celery
- 1 red bell pepper
- 50 g sugar snap peas
- 7.5 ml sesame oil
- 10 g cashew nuts
- 15 g sesame seeds
- 100 g tofu
- 7.5 ml soy sauce
- 7.5 ml vegan fish sauce

Preparation:

1. To cook the rice, go to the package instructions.
2. After cleaning, slice the spring onions into rings.
3. Trim, cut, and wash the celery.
4. Peel, core, and seed the bell pepper.
5. Slice the sugar snap peas into strips after washing.
6. Stirring frequently, fry the vegetables in the heated oil for three to four minutes.
7. In a pan without oil, briskly toast the cashew nuts and sesame seeds.
8. Chop the tofu and incorporate it with the vegetables and grains.
9. To taste, add the chili powder, soy sauce, and fish sauce.
10. Transfer to two bowls and reheat for a further two minutes.
11. Before serving, sprinkle with the sesame seed mixture.

Nutritional information per serving:

- 395 kcal
- Carbohydrates: 55 g

- Fat: 12 g
- -Protein: 17 g

65. Colorful salad bowl with tahini dressing

Ingredients for 2 portions:

- 2 carrots
- 1 cucumber
- 10 cherry tomatoes
- 100 g rocket
- 1 zucchini
- 6 radishes
- 2 spring onions
- 15 g tahini
- 2-3 tablespoons olive oil
- Salt, pepper
- 50 ml water
- 15 g balsamic vinegar
- 2 strawberries
- Fresh coriander

Preparation:

1. Make the rocket clean.
2. Grate the carrots finely after washing.
3. Slice the cucumber thinly after washing.
4. Cut the tomatoes in half after washing.
5. After cleaning, chop the zucchini into pieces.
6. After washing, thinly slice the radishes.
7. After cleaning, slice the spring onions into rings.
8. Halve, peel, and quarter the strawberries.
9. 15 grams of tahini, 2 to 3 tablespoons olive oil, 2 to 3 tablespoons water, balsamic vinegar, salt, and pepper should all be well combined in a big dish.
10. Mix well after adding the dressing to the vegetables.
11. After washing the rocket, put it in a bowl with the veggies, top with

strawberries and coriander, and serve.

Nutritional information per serving:

- 217 kcal
- Carbohydrates: 6g
- Fat: 13 g
- Protein: 4 g

66. Rice bowl with fried vegetables

Ingredients for 2 portions:

- 125 g basmati rice
- ½ Courgette
- ½ stalk of leek
- 150 g green beans
- 1 red bell pepper
- 1 tomato
- 1 garlic clove
- 15 g peanuts
- 15 g fried onions
- 15 g rapeseed oil
- 7.5 ml rice vinegar
- 15 g soy sauce
- Salt, pepper, sugar

Preparation:

1. To cook the rice, go to the package instructions.
2. Slice the zucchini after giving them a wash.
3. After peeling, split the leek into rings.
4. Boil the beans for six minutes in salted water after washing.
5. Peel, core, and seed the bell pepper.
6. Cut the tomatoes into tiny pieces after washing.
7. In a mortar, crush the peanuts and fried onions.
8. Finely cut and peel the garlic.
9. Garlic is sautéed in rapeseed oil in a wok until it becomes transparent.
10. Stir-fry the bell pepper and leek for 2 minutes on high heat.
11. To the wok, add the beans, tomatoes, and zucchini.
12. Add vinegar, soy sauce, sugar, salt, and pepper to taste.

Nutritional information per serving:

- 447 kcal

- Carbohydrates: 51 g
- Fat: 21 g
- Protein: 12 g

67. Broccoli and pumpkin bowl

Ingredients for 2 portions:

- 150 g buckwheat
- 1 carrot
- Vegetable broth
- 250 g pumpkin
- ½ red onion
- 2 7.5 ml olive oil
- Salt, pepper, chili powder
- 400 g broccoli
- 10 g mixed herbs
- 2 tablespoons cashew nuts
- 20 g green olives
- 30 g capers
- ¼ lemon, squeezed
- 30 g miso paste
- 4 ml honey

Preparation:

1. After cleaning, cook for 20 to 25 minutes in 325 milliliters of stock.
2. Carrots should be peeled, chopped into cubes, and then added to the buckwheat for ten minutes.
3. After peeling, chop the pumpkin into 1.5 cm pieces.
4. After peeling, thinly slice the onion into rings.
5. Two teaspoons of oil should be heated in a skillet. After the onion rings are transparent, add the pumpkin and continue to cook for five minutes.
6. Use 50 ml of stock to deglaze, then cover and simmer for 12 to 15 minutes.
7. Broccoli should be cleaned, sliced into florets, then cooked for five minutes to make it al dente.
8. After washing, pat dry, and remove any leaves from the herbs.

9. Chop the capers, olives, and cashew nuts coarsely.
10. Combine the lemon juice with ½ tablespoon of oil, chili powder, honey, miso paste, 5–6 tablespoons of stock, salt, and pepper.
11. Top the buckwheat with the broccoli and pumpkin, then drizzle with the sauce and top with the cashew and herb combination.

Nutritional information per serving:

- 531 kcal
- Carbohydrates: 70 g
- Fat: 20 g
- Protein: 16 g

68. Winter bowl with nut-orange dressing

Ingredients for 2 portions:

- 125 g basmati rice
- 50 g lamb's lettuce
- 100 g red cabbage
- 1 ½ onions Beetroot
- 15 g walnuts
- 10 g pistachios
- 1 Orange
- 30 ml walnut oil
- 7.5 ml white wine vinegar
- 15 g nut butter
- Salt, pepper, thyme

Preparation:

1. To cook the rice, go to the package instructions.
2. Shake dry the lettuce from the rinsed lamb.
3. Slice the red cabbage thinly after washing.
4. The beet should be sliced into strips.
5. In a skillet without any fat, roast the nuts and seeds, then chop.
6. After inserting a filter halfway into the orange and gathering the juice, squeeze the remaining liquid out.
7. Stir the oil, vinegar, orange juice, and nut butter together, then mix in half of the nut and seed combination. Garnish with thyme, salt, and pepper.
8. Spoon the rice, beet, red cabbage, lamb's lettuce, orange fillets, and leftover nut and seed combination into each of two dishes; pour over the sauce.

Nutritional information per serving:

- 513 kcal
- Carbohydrates: 66 g
- Fat: 21 g

- Protein: 12 g

Ingredients for 2 portions:

- 80 g lighter quinoa
- 5 ml vegetable stock
- 200 g sweet potatoes
- ½ fresh beet
- 60 g walnuts
- 25 g sunflower seeds
- Salt, pepper
- 15 g olive oil
- 2 handfuls of baby spinach
- ½ jar kidney beans
- ½ ripe avocado
- 4 stalks of fresh mint
- Juice of ½ lemon
- 2 tablespoons tahini

Preparation:

1. To prepare the quinoa, adhere to the directions provided on the package.
2. After peeling and chopping, arrange the sweet potatoes on a baking dish covered with parchment paper.
3. After that, bake for 20 to 25 minutes at 180 °C in a preheated oven.
4. Blend the beet till it's crumbly and somewhat sticky, adding walnuts, sunflower seeds, olive oil, and five milligrams of salt.
5. To dry the spinach, give it a thorough rinse and shake.
6. Let the kidney beans drain and rinse.
7. Clean the mint, remove the leaves, and finely chop.
8. After peeling the avocado, cut the flesh into slices.
9. Add salt and pepper to the quinoa to season it.
10. Split the avocado, crumbled beet, quinoa, sweet potatoes, spinach, and walnuts between two bowls. Add some tahini drizzle and season

with salt, pepper, vinegar, and lemon juice.

Nutritional information per serving:

- 830 kcal
- Carbohydrates: 66 g
- Fat: 50 g
- Protein: 22 g

70. Rice bowl with avocado

Ingredients for 2 portions:
- 75 g wholegrain rice
- Salt, pepper
- 50 ml vegetable stock
- 20 g coconut cream
- 30 g peanut butter
- 7.5 ml soy sauce
- 2.5 g coconut blossom sugar
- 15 g lime juice
- 125 g tofu
- 15 g peanut oil
- 40 g peanuts
- 150 g carrots
- 50 g baby spinach
- 100 g blueberries
- 1 avocado

Preparation:
1. To cook the rice, go to the package instructions.
2. Stir in the peanut butter after bringing the coconut cream and vegetable stock to a boil.
3. Add the soy sauce, lime juice, coconut blossom sugar, salt, and pepper and stir to create a smooth sauce.

4. Fry the tofu in a skillet over medium heat, cutting it into ½ cm cubes.
5. Without using any oil, roast the peanuts over medium heat.
6. After peeling and slicing, the carrots are cut diagonally into thin sticks.
7. Shake out any excess water from the spinach.
8. Clean the blueberries.
9. Halve the avocado lengthwise and take out the pit. Take the meat out of the skin.
10. Transfer the chilled rice into dishes and garnish with blueberries, peanuts, avocado, carrots, spinach, and tofu. Add a little peanut sauce drizzle.

Nutritional information per serving:
- 678 kcal
- Carbohydrates: 46 g
- Fat: 42 g
- Protein: 27 g

Chapter 8: Frequently Asked Questions About Bowl Diets

The bowl diet has been extremely popular in recent years because it provides a flexible and easy way to eat healthily. The popularity of the bowl diet fad is rising as more and more individuals seek out quick meals that are also packed with nutrition. The most common queries concerning the bowl diet are addressed in this comprehensive guide. We examine the advantages of the bowl diet as well as any possible risks, and we offer suggestions for preparing tasty, well-balanced bowl meals.

1. **What is a bowl diet?**

A bowl diet is a type of eating plan in which participants are encouraged to construct their meals using a bowl and a range of different items. Bowl diets are becoming increasingly popular now. Components of the diet that are typically included include vegetables, lean proteins, unsaturated fats, grains, and various forms of complex carbs and healthy fats among other things. In addition to being nutritious, the objective should be to develop cuisine that is not only visually beautiful but also offers a wide range of nutrients in a single serving.

2. **What are the benefits of a bowl diet?**

- *Bowl diets encourage the eating of a wide variety of nutrients because a bowl can contain a variety of components. This facilitates the ingestion of a wide range of nutrients.*

- *Control of portions: The bowls naturally restrict the size of portions, encourage individuals to eat in a thoughtful manner, and assist individuals in controlling the amount of calories they consume.*

- *Personalization: Bowl diets are extremely customizable, enabling individuals to personalize their meals to specific dietary choices, constraints, or health goals. Bowl diets are also known as "bowl diets."*

- *Bowl dinners are convenient since they are simple to prepare and require almost no prior experience in the kitchen. They are therefore a sensible option for individuals who lead hectic lifestyles because of this.*

3. **Are bowl diets suitable for weight loss?**

Certainly, bowl diets have the potential to be beneficial for weight loss if they are implemented with the management of volume and food density in mind. The production of satiating meals that are conducive to weight loss can be accomplished by the utilization of lean protein, a variety of vegetables, and whole grains in culinary dishes. On the other hand, it is essential to pay attention to the sizes of the portions and to steer clear of excessive amounts of toppings or dressings that are high in calories.

4. **Can bowl diets cover the nutritional requirements?**

Shellfish nutrition has the potential to fulfill all of the body's nutritional requirements if it is ingested along with the appropriate dosage. The consumption of a well-balanced combination of macronutrients (proteins, fats, and carbs) and micronutrients for optimal health is of utmost importance (vitamins and minerals). A diet that includes a wide variety of veggies, lean meats, healthy fats, and whole grains as well as a colorful assortment of these foods can guarantee that you consume a wide range of essential nutrients.

5. **How can I prepare a balanced bowl meal?**

To prepare a balanced bowl meal, you should follow the tips below:

- Lean proteins, such as grilled chicken, tofu, beans, or fish, should be included in the ingredient list.
- Add a half of your bowl to colorful veggies that are rich in fiber, vitamins, and minerals. Fill the other half of your bowl with vegetables.
- Choose whole grain items like quinoa or brown rice for prolonged energy. Carbohydrates: Choose goods that contain whole grains.
- Fats that are good for you: Include foods that contain healthy fats, such as olive oil, avocados, and almonds.
- Make your bowl more flavorful by adding herbs, spices, and healthy sauces to it. This will help you avoid consuming an excessive amount of calories.

6. **Are bowl diets suitable for vegetarians or vegans?**

So, in any event. It is not difficult to include a vegan or vegetarian meal into a bowl diet because of its adaptability and versatility. Some examples of plant-based proteins that can be excellent sources of nutrients in a bowl meal include tofu, tempeh, lentils, and grains. These are just a few different examples. Not only should a vegetarian or vegan bowl contain a variety of veggies, but it should also contain lipids derived from plants in order to be considered complete and satisfying.

7. **Can the bowl diets meet dietary restrictions or allergies?**

It is true that bowl diets are able to accommodate a wide range of dietary restrictions and allergies in a method that is both straightforward and handy. It is still possible for individuals to have bowl meals that are both delicious and nutritious through the selection of components that are tailored to their specific dietary requirements. As an illustration, those who are sensitive to gluten have the choice of selecting gluten-free grains such as quinoa, while individuals who are allergic to dairy have the option of selecting alternatives that do not include dairy proteins.

8. **What mistakes should I avoid when preparing bowl dishes?**

- Overindulgence in consumption Caution should be exercised with regard to portion proportions, particularly when it comes to high-calorie items like nuts, oils, and sauces.
- Protein deficiency: Ensure that your dish has an adequate quantity of protein to maintain satiety and the preservation of muscular mass.
- Don't bother with it: When searching for a diversified nutritional profile, it is important to look for a diversity of colors and textures.
- Inputs that have been overly processed: Reduce the amount of highly processed or sugary items you use in your diet to achieve the best possible health advantages.

Conclusion

As a result of the fact that we have arrived at the end of the final segment of the culinary journey that is described in The Bowls Cookbook, there is now time to reflect, rejoice, and even experience a few feelings of sentimentality. There is a universe that has been revealed within the pages of this cookbook, in which bowls are not only containers for food; rather, they are the very essence of a lifestyle that is both healthier and more delicious. This universe has been revealed. According to your point of view, what are some of the things that we ought to take away from our culinary journey? It is the intention of this article to persuade individuals that the skill of bowl-centric cooking is not merely a passing fad, but rather a significant shift toward the nutritional benefits, ease of preparation, and gourmet pleasure that it can bring about.

Over the course of the previous pages, we have talked about the difficulties that a significant number of us face on a daily basis. The constant ticking of the clock, the struggle to find a balance between health and convenience, and the desire for meals that not only satisfy our need for fuel but also excite our taste buds are some of the challenges that we face during this time. Not only has The Bowls Cookbook acknowledged these problems, but it has also eliminated them, one meal at a time, by providing a solution that is not only delicious but also practical. With this cookbook, you can eliminate these problems.

A bowl is more than just a container; rather, it is a canvas for creativity, a palette on which colors, flavors, and textures can mix to create a symphony of flavor. This cookbook is built on the premise that a bowl is more than just a container. This idea is not only straightforward but also revolutionary. The entire cookbook is based on this fundamental idea, which serves as its foundation. In other words, it is about coming to terms with the fact that a dinner can be a celebration of food while also being easy to make in a short amount of time. This is something that needs to be acknowledged. The purpose of this cookbook is to serve as both a guide and a companion, but more importantly, it demonstrates that eating healthily does not have to be restricted in any way; rather, it can be a source of pleasure.

Take a few moments to reflect on some of the most significant ideas that we have discussed up to this point in time because they are important. During the process of selecting each and every recipe that is included in this book, the principles of bowl cooking have been taken into consideration. This includes the energizing breakfast bowls that will provide you with a wonderful beginning to the day, as well as the full dinners that will provide you with a satisfying conclusion to the day. Both of these options are included in this. The importance of achieving taste harmony, the satisfaction of preparing a meal that not only nourishes the body but also puts a smile on your face, and the significance of recognizing the significance of maintaining a healthy balance between various nutrients are all topics that we have discussed in the past.

In contrast, this cookbook is not merely a collection of recipes; rather, it is a compilation of a great deal more than that. It is a guide that will show you how to become the conductor of a symphony of flavors in your kitchen, one that is in tune with your individual preferences and the objectives you have established for your health. Cooking with bowls is a skill that can be applied to a wider variety of situations than just the recipes themselves, and you will learn both the art and the science of cooking with bowls throughout the course of these pages. Having an understanding of the alchemy of materials, the dance of flavors, and the excitement of cooking meals that are not only a celebration of life but also the act of providing for one's own sustenance is what it means to have this understanding.

The next topic that we are going to talk about is promises, so let's move on to that. What did you anticipate finding on the very first page of this cookbook when you first opened the cover and turned the page? It is possible that it was the answer to the age-old problem of finding a balance between one's personal life and one's professional life. It is possible that you were looking for new ideas to experiment with in the kitchen that would not require an excessive amount of time from your already packed schedule. If this is the case, then you are in the right place. In light of the fact that we are now saying our goodbyes, it is time to contemplate whether or not The Bowls Cookbook has fulfilled its promise of providing you with a method of cooking in your kitchen that is not only convenient but also delicious.

This is your culinary report card; it is a representation of the fact that each and every meal, each and every piece of advice, and each and every insight that is presented in these pages has been produced with the specific intention of delivering on that promise. Imagine this as your culinary report card. Here, we are not going to take a cookie-cutter approach; rather, we are going to provide you with the resources, information, and inspiration you require in order to make cooking around the bowl a truly individual experience for you. It is possible that this promise will be fulfilled if, after reading these pages, you come to the realization that you value the versatility and convenience that bowls provide.

As the person who is currently reading "Bowls Cookbook," what is the one thing that I would like you to take away from the experience of reading this book? A bowl is more than just a container for food; rather, it is a container for transformation. This idea has to do with the realization that a bowl is more than just a container for food. The core of this idea is this realization that has just occurred. On this canvas, ordinary ingredients can be transformed into outstanding dishes, convenience and health can coexist, and the joy of cooking can be reimagined. It is a canvas that can be used to transform ordinary ingredients into outstanding dishes. Each and every one of these things is attainable through the utilization of standard components. I would like you to keep in mind that nourishment for your body does not have to be a burden, but rather an act of self-love, and that each dish that you cook has the potential to be a step towards a better and happier version of yourself. I would like you to keep this in mind. Whenever you go somewhere, you should make sure to bring this information with you. What I want you to do is that.

Remember that even if you succeed in finishing this book, you have not yet arrived at the destination of your journey. This is something you should keep in mind. You can think of The Bowls Cookbook as more than just a collection of recipes; it serves as a springboard for your exploration of the fascinating world of culinary arts. You are about to embark on an adventure into the vast and wonderful world of flavors, and you should allow the fundamentals of bowl cooking to serve as your guide. You should make an effort to experiment with new things, think creatively, and most importantly, take pleasure in each and every moment that you spend in the kitchen.

I would like to raise a glass to the bowls that have already left your table as you have worked your way through the recipes contained in this volume. I would also like to raise a glass to the many bowls that are still to come. In addition to the joy that comes from eating, may they also experience the pleasure of tasting each meal, the satisfaction that comes from creating something, and the joy that comes from maintaining something. May they be blessed with all of these things. The journey toward a life that is both healthier and more appetizing is not merely a destination; rather, it is a delectable adventure that unfolds with each bowl that you prepare as you enter your kitchen with the information and inspiration that you have gained from these pages. It is important to keep this in mind because it is a journey that is not simply a destination. As I raise a glass to the Bowls Cookbook, which is an adventure across the world of meals, I would like to take this opportunity to thank you. It is my sincere wish that this marks the beginning of a lifetime of great pleasure in the kitchen, as well as the beginning of a multitude of delicious dinners.

Made in the USA
Middletown, DE
22 November 2024

65189129R00064